MACHINES THAT WON THE WAR

MACHINES AND WEAPONRY OF THE COLD WAR

Charlie Samuels

Gareth Stevens
Publishing

Please visit our website, www.garethstevens.com. For a free color catalog of all our high-quality books, call toll free 1-800-542-2595 or fax 1-877-542-2596.

Library of Congress Cataloging-in-Publication Data

Samuels, Charlie, 1961-
 Machines and weaponry of the Cold War / Charlie Samuels.
    p. cm. — (Machines that won the war)
 Includes index.
 ISBN 978-1-4339-8592-8 (pbk.)
 ISBN 978-1-4339-8593-5 (6-pack)
 ISBN 978-1-4339-8591-1 (library binding)
 1. Weapons systems—United States—History—20th century. 2. United States—Armed Forces—Equipment—History—20th century. 3. Cold War. I. Title.
 UF503.S36 2013
 623.40973'09045—dc23
                        2012037841

ISBN: 978-1-4339-8592-8 (paperback)
ISBN: 978-1-4339-8591-1 (hardcover)

Published in 2013 by
Gareth Stevens Publishing
111 East 14th Street, Suite 349
New York, NY 10003

© 2013 Brown Bear Books Ltd.

For Brown Bear Books Ltd:
Editorial Director: Lindsey Lowe
Managing Editor: Tim Cooke
Children's Publisher: Anne O'Daly
Art Director: Jeni Child
Designer: Lynne Lennon
Picture Manager: Sophie Mortimer
Production Director: Alastair Gourlay

Picture Credits
Front Cover: U.S. Department of Defense

All photographs U.S. Department of Defense except: **BAe Ltd**: 20; **Alan Denney**: 34;
RIA Novosti: 43tr; **Shutterstock**: Paul Drabot 18, Stephen Meese 45tr; **Thinkstock**: Hemera 35tl, iStockphoto 8.

Key: t = top, c = center, b = bottom, l = left, r = right.

Manufactured in the United States of America
1 2 3 4 5 6 7 8 9 12 11 10

CPSIA compliance information: Batch #CW13GS: For further information contact Gareth Stevens, New York, New York at 1-800-542-2595.

CONTENTS

INTRODUCTION

A fter World War II ended in 1945, the world split into two camps. The United States and its allies supported democracy and free trade. The Soviet Union, which controlled much of eastern Europe, promoted communism and state control. The clash between the two ideologies is called the Cold War. It lasted from the late 1940s until the fall of the Soviet Union in 1991.

A Tomahawk cruise missile streaks away from USS *Missouri*. In the Cold War, long-range missiles were the most important form of weapon.

Ideology: A system of political ideas that forms the basis of a society.

U.S. military personnel watch a nuclear explosion in the Nevada desert in 1951. At the time, the dangers of nuclear fallout were not entirely understood, so the men are standing too close for safety.

IN THE SHADOW OF THE BOMB

The Cold War never erupted into open warfare between the two major powers. But there were smaller wars in which each side tried to weaken the other by supporting and arming one set of combatants or the other.

The introduction of nuclear weapons in 1945 cast a shadow over the Cold War. Atomic bombs could destroy whole nations. Battlefield weapons became less important than strategic weapons aimed at preventing an enemy from attacking. Submarines, missiles, and aircraft were the chief means by which the struggle was waged.

Fallout: The spread of harmful microscopic nuclear material after an atomic explosion.

B-47 STRATOJET

The B-47 was designed near the end of World War II. It was intended to be a long-range bomber that could fly from the United States to bomb Germany. During the Cold War, the jet became the standard medium bomber of the U.S. Air Force. More than 2,000 were built. They carried nuclear bombs that could be dropped on the Soviet Union.

Smoke blasts from the back of a B-47 as it uses rocket power for a quick takeoff. The pods beneath the wings carried additional fuel.

Nuclear: A bomb that works by releasing the vast power contained in atoms.

Swept wings first appeared on the B-47 Stratojet. Engineers realized that the shape was more efficient than traditional straight wings, allowing the jet to get more speed out of its power.

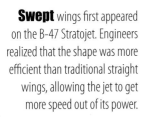

A B-47 pilot communicates with ground crew before takeoff. The airplane's remarkable range meant that it could get from U.S. bases to virtually anywhere in the world.

EYEWITNESS

"I can't say enough good things about it. I loved it! I didn't know anyone who flew it who didn't fall in love with it. It was a good, safe airplane."

Lloyd Griffin
B-47 pilot

INNOVATIVE DESIGN

The B-47 flew at high altitudes at high subsonic speeds. It had an innovative design. Its swept wings were new. They were angled backward. Straight wings would not allow the aircraft to use the full power of the engines. Today swept wings are standard: All modern airplanes are descended from the B-47.

The jet had a crew of three, and a maximum speed of 607 miles per hour (977 km/h). Its range could be up to 10,000 miles (16,100 km). As well as being a bomber, the B-47 could take photos, carry out electronic surveillance, and gather data about the weather. It was never used as a bomber.

Swept wing: A wing that is angled back on either side, creating a roughly triangular shape.

CENTURION TANK

The British developed the Centurion during World War II, but too late for it to see combat. During the Cold War, it was popular with armies across the world. It was officially a cruiser tank, so it was fast and mobile. But it had the firepower of a much heavier tank. The combination helped keep the Centurion in production until the 1990s.

The main gun of the Centurion was originally a 17-pounder (76mm) gun; it later became the more powerful L7 105mm gun.

Firepower: The amount of offensive weapons, such as guns or cannon, a vehicle possesses.

Centurions firing at nighttime use tracer shells coated with chemicals that glow to show their path in the dark.

HEAVY GUNS

Tanks played an important role in frontline maneuvers. They were constantly being upgraded. The Centurion's guns became bigger and its armor became thicker. Tasks such as aiming at a target became computerized.

The Centurion was used in many smaller military clashes in the Cold War. British troops used it in the Korean War (1950–1953), while Israel used it in conflicts with Soviet-backed Arab states in the 1960s and 1970s. The Centurion was such a successful main battle tank that there are more versions of it than of any other main battle tank.

T-64 TANK

The main Soviet response to Western tanks was the T-64 medium tank, which appeared in 1966. It was well armored. Its innovations included an automatic loader for its 125mm gun: that meant one crewmember less in its cramped cabin! The T-64 became the basis of modern Soviet tanks.

Maneuvers: The coordinated positioning and moving around of military forces.

9

CRUISE MISSILE

A cruise missile is any kind of self-propelled bomb that can fly—"cruise"—for long distances before striking its target with deadly accuracy. It has three key parts: a guidance system, a warhead, and a propulsion system or engine. The first cruise missiles were made by Germany during World War II. These "flying bombs" were not very accurate and had a short range. By the Cold War, there had been great advances in missile technology.

Flames blaze as a cruise missile is fired from the deck of a U.S. warship. The missiles can be fired from land, from the air, from a surface ship, or from a submerged submarine.

Guidance system: The part of a missile that steers it toward the target.

A Tomahawk cruise missile flies above mountains in California shortly after being launched in 1980.

A missile blasts a warehouse during an exercise. The missiles are usually aimed at "high value" targets, such as ships, transportation links, or command and control centers.

A NEW THREAT

The cruise missile could travel at sub- or supersonic speeds, and strike at short or very long range. It could carry conventional or nuclear bombs. Later missiles could be steered to their targets by a computer. Others hug the shape of the landscape as they fly just above it.

The U.S. Army's first surface-to-surface cruise missile was the MGM-1 Matador. It was based in Germany during the Cold War. It was capable of striking any of the countries in the Warsaw Pact.

POWER BLOCS

During the Cold War, many nations joined alliances for greater security. The United States and its European allies formed the North Atlantic Treaty Organization (NATO). In response, the Soviet Union and its allies formed an alliance called the Warsaw Pact.

Supersonic: Traveling faster than the speed of sound, 768 miles per hour (1,236 km/h).

More than 5,000 Phantoms were built in various models before production ended in 1979.

F-4 PHANTOM

The F-4 Phantom entered service in 1961. The twin-seat fighter–bomber could carry nuclear missiles or conventional bombs. It worked in "hunter-killer" teams of two. The planes detected and located enemy radar, then directed their weapons at the target. The Phantom was called the "world's leading distributor of MiG parts" because it destroyed so many Soviet-built MiG jets.

EYEWITNESS

"Only in the F-4 Phantom have I had the freedom to indulge in my every fantasy. I only have to think 'Speed,' and I am at 600 knots in seconds. Think 'Height' and I am gazing down from an eight-mile-high perch within one minute." **Robert Prest RAF Fighter Pilot**

Twin seat: An aircraft with two cockpits, both of which have the full range of controls.

During an exercise, a policeman in chemical warfare clothing guards an F-4 Phantom; the pilot sits in the front cockpit, with a weapons systems officer in the rear cockpit.

OUTSTANDING PERFORMANCE

The Phantom is still in use today, thanks to its technical abilities. The supersonic airplane can fly at twice the speed of sound, or Mach 2: over 1,600 miles per hour (2,575 km/h). It can fly at an altitude of 60,000 feet (18,288 m) and has a range of 1,300 miles (2,090 km). It has broken world records for the highest and fastest flights.

The Phantom carries more than 18,000 pounds (8,165 kg) of weapons. It tracks targets using its Pave Tack system. The Pave Tack is carried in a pod beneath the aircraft. It uses laser and infrared to designate targets for the weapons and to guide them home.

F-4 Phantoms fly in formation with F-15 Eagles during an operation in 1981.

Altitude: The height above the ground at which an airplane can fly.

F-15 EAGLE

The F-15 Eagle was the world's most successful fighter jet. It was designed to fight the Russian MiG jet. Its ratio of air-to-air combat "kills" was an amazing 104–0. For more than 30 years, it was the king of the skies. The pilots who flew it loved its design: It was fast, powerful, easy to maneuver, and had a long range.

These F-15s are armed with Sidewinder and AIM-7 Sparrow missiles carried on the pylons beneath their wings.

Air-to-air combat: Fighting between two aircraft in flight.

The thrust of the F-15's twin engines is far greater than its weight, enabling it to accelerate into a vertical climb.

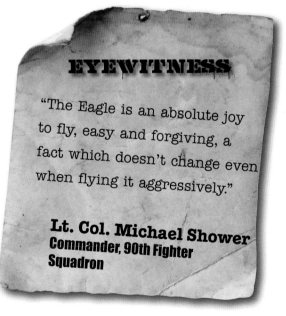

EYEWITNESS

"The Eagle is an absolute joy to fly, easy and forgiving, a fact which doesn't change even when flying it aggressively."

Lt. Col. Michael Shower
Commander, 90th Fighter Squadron

A SUPER JET

The Eagle entered U.S. Air Force service in 1976. It was the most advanced fighter of its day. It could quickly scare away enemy aircraft to win control of the skies.

The Eagle's powerful engines allowed the plane to take off almost vertically. Its wings were bigger than on most fast jets. That gave the pilot more maneuverability. The cockpit was full of new technology, like the hands-on throttle and stick (HOTAS). Buttons on the joystick allowed the pilot to control weapons and other systems without letting go of the stick.

Joystick: The column that controls the height and direction of an airplane.

The Sabre is the most produced of all Western jet fighters; 9,860 planes were built.

F-86 SABRE

The Sabre, a single-seat fighter-bomber, was a favorite of U.S. Air Force pilots. It was effective, but it was also innovative. It was the first swept wing aircraft to be constructed. At the end of World War II (1939–1945), the Americans seized German technical data. The data showed that a swept wing would absorb shock waves, enabling a plane to go faster without shaking apart. U.S. engineers produced the Sabre in time for the Korean War (1950–1953).

Fighter-bomber: An airplane that can attack other aircraft in the air or targets on the ground.

Lieutenant Colonel Richard F. Turner was one of the aces of the 4th Fighter Interceptor Wing in Korea.

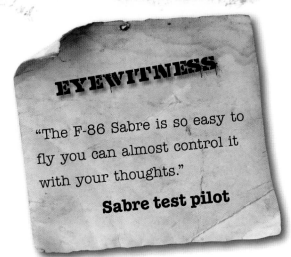
A restored Sabre banks into a turn during an air show.

KOREAN VICTOR

The war in Korea saw the last major air battles in warfare. Later in the Cold War, air-to-air missiles took over. The Sabre's record against Soviet MiGs in Korea was outstanding. For every Sabre that was downed, seven MiGs were shot down.

The Sabre had a top speed of 675 miles per hour (1,085 km/h) and it reached an altitude of 48,300 feet (14,722 m). It was fast and easy to maneuver, and was armed with six machine guns.

Ace: A pilot who has shot down a certain number of enemy aircraft.

HARRIER

Versions of the Harrier have been in use for over 40 years, since its introduction by Britain's Royal Air Force (RAF) in 1969. It was the world's first operational fixed-wing vertical take-off and landing (VTOL) strike-fighter. It could rise straight from the ground, like a helicopter, and then fly as a conventional jet.

The Harrier took just 2 minutes 22 seconds to fly to an altitude of 40,000 feet (12,200 m) from vertical takeoff.

Fixed wing: Wings that remain in one position, unlike the rotating blades of a helicopter.

Harriers come in to land on a carrier. They were armed with 30mm guns, and carried bombs and rockets.

ROTATING ENGINES

Helicopters and jets used rotors or direct thrust, respectively, to take off. The Harrier's Pegasus engine had four nozzles that could rotate. To take off or land, they swung into a vertical position. A VTOL aircraft did not need a runway. That made it very flexible. It could be launched from small airfields or aircraft carriers. A special carrier version, the Sea Harrier, was launched in 1980. It fought in the Falklands War between Britain and Argentina in 1982. It shot down 20 enemy jets in return for one Harrier lost.

EYEWITNESS

"It required all the skill that I could bring to bear in terms of handling the aeroplane. That's what test flying was like in the 1960s—there were no simulators."

John Farley
Original RAF test pilot, 1964

Sea Harriers wait to take off from an aircraft carrier during the Falklands War.

Aircraft carrier: A warship with a flat deck to allow airplanes to take off and land.

The Lightning was the first airplane capable of "super-cruise," or spending long periods at supersonic speeds.

ENGLISH ELECTRIC
LIGHTNING

Pilots said that flying the Lightning was like being strapped to a rocket. The Lightning was the first British jet to fly at twice the speed of sound, Mach 2. It achieved that feat in 1958. The speed that earned its "Lightning" name also made the airplane a great interceptor.

Interceptor: A fighter that can interrupt the flight of an enemy aircraft.

RACEHORSE OF THE SKIES

The Lightning could also climb to altitude super fast. After take off, it could shoot up almost vertically. It could reach 40,000 feet (12,200 m) in just two minutes. Such power used a lot of fuel, so the airplane's range was short. At supersonic speed, it could only fly for 850 miles (1,370 km). Its wings were swept back to allow it to accelerate fast.

The "racehorse of the skies" was popular. Pilots loved to fly it. During the Cold War it was scrambled in order to turn back Soviet reconnaissance aircraft that were headed for Great Britain. A total of 337 Lightnings were built. But despite its popularity, the aircraft turned out to be the last British supersonic fighter to be manufactured.

EYEWITNESS

"For the pure joy of flying, the Lightning still heads the list. It was and still is a magnificent aircraft, and a credit to the designers and test pilots who developed and brought it into service for people like me to enjoy."

Brian Carroll
Wing Commander, RAF

Air enthusiasts watch a Lightning takeoff in the 1960s armed with air-to-air missiles.

Scramble: To get pilots into aircraft and the aircraft off the ground very quickly.

LOS ANGELES CLASS SUBMARINE

The Los Angeles class was a class of nuclear-powered fast-attack submarines. Built from 1972 to 1996, the Los Angeles class is still the backbone of the U.S. Navy. Of the 62 built, 42 vessels are still in service. One of their jobs is to patrol the world's oceans carrying Tomahawk cruise missiles. The Tomahawk can be fired from deep beneath the sea at a target up to 1,550 miles (2,500 km) away.

The USS *City of Corpus Christi* cruises on the surface; the Los Angeles class submarines can travel at speeds of 20 knots (23 miles per hour; 37 km/h).

Fast-attack: A type of submarine designed to strike at enemy vessels.

22

The crew of a new Los Angeles class submarine stand at attention on its superstructure as it is launched down a slipway into the water.

The command deck of a Los Angeles submarine is cramped—like the whole vessel; there are 129 people on board.

SUB HUNTER

Los Angeles class vessels were designed to have other functions. One of the most important was to protect aircraft carriers and other warships from enemy submarines. It uses radar to track enemy vessels and torpedoes to attack them.

In addition to its fighting capacity, the sub has many other uses. It can gather intelligence, deliver Special Forces to remote places, lay mines, and carry out search-and-rescue missions. They can even travel beneath the polar ice caps, and remain underwater for 90 days.

EYEWITNESS

"Our biggest threat is another submarine. Our best defense against enemy subs will be tactics, training, and motivation. The crew that acts first and makes the fewest mistakes will win."

Executive Officer
U.S. Los Angeles class sub

Torpedo: An underwater missile that has its own engine to push it through the water.

M1 ABRAMS

The political tensions of the Cold War inspired many technological advances. Both superpowers tried to get an advantage over the other. One of the areas of biggest advance was the tank. Tanks became bigger. Their guns were more powerful and their armor was thicker. The M-1 Abrams entered service in 1980 as the main battle tank of the U.S. Army and the Marine Corps.

The M1 Abrams had a crew of four: commander, driver, loader, and gunner.

Superpowers: The countries that led the Cold War: the United States and the Soviet Union.

A **member** of an M1 Abrams crew keeps watch with the .50 caliber (12.7mm) heavy machine gun that is the tank's main secondary armament.

A POPULAR GUN

The M1 was covered in laminate Chobam armor to protect it from a new battlefield threat: missiles. The M1 carried a 105mm main gun with a kill range of 8,200 feet (2,500 m). That was much further than its Soviet counterpart. The U.S. tank could hit the enemy before it was within the enemy's range. Its acceleration and top speed were also superior to enemy tanks.

The tank was high-tech. A fire-control computer calculated the range of the target and the angle of fire, so that its shells were fired as accurately as possible.

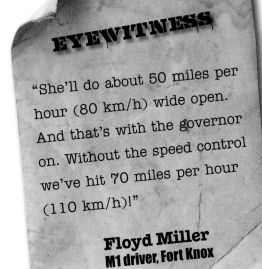

EYEWITNESS

"She'll do about 50 miles per hour (80 km/h) wide open. And that's with the governor on. Without the speed control we've hit 70 miles per hour (110 km/h)!"

Floyd Miller
M1 driver, Fort Knox

Laminate: A hard material made by combining thin layers of metal and ceramic.

USS NIMITZ

The Nimitz class are super-carriers. The 10 nuclear-powered aircraft carriers are the largest and most powerful warships ever built. They were built in the mid-1970s. Combat aircraft were getting heavier, so carriers needed longer flight decks. On the *Nimitz*, the flight deck is 1,092 feet (333 m) long and 252 feet (79 m) wide. A Nimitz-class carrier can carry as many as 90 aircraft. It is the size of a small town. The ship's crew is more than 5,000 people.

Ship's personnel *"man the rails" of the USS Nimitz as it is towed out of port ready to begin a mission.*

Class: A group of warships that are all based on the same design and specifications.

This aerial photograph shows the USS *Nimitz* underway, with aircraft arranged around its flight deck.

Sea Stallion helicopters are stored in a hangar beneath the deck of USS *Nimitz*; the helicopters' rotors fold to make them fit better.

MULTITASKER

The first carrier in the class, USS *Nimitz*, was deployed to the Indian Ocean in 1980. Radicals in Iran had taken U.S. personnel hostage in the capital, Tehran. The ship filled the role of a floating airbase during the crisis. The carriers are used to carry out sea and air blockades, to make missile strikes, and to lay minefields.

Nimitz-class vessels can stay at sea for an amazing 13 years. It runs on nuclear power, so it does not need to refuel. It just needs supply ships to bring provisions for the crew. The USS *Dwight D. Eisenhower* set a record in 1980 by staying at sea for 152 days without visiting port.

FLOATING TOWN

A Nimitz-class carrier is like a small town. Its cooks serve up to 20,000 meals a day. The barber trims 1,500 heads a week. There's a 53-bed hospital on board and one multi-faith chapel. Fresh water is distilled every day, and the ship carries food supplies for up to 10 weeks.

Hostage: Someone who is held against their will for a particular purpose.

NUCLEAR BOMB

One weapon dominated the Cold War: the atomic bomb. People often just referred to it as "the bomb." The nuclear bombs dropped on Japan at the end of World War II in 1945 showed how powerful the weapons were. People were terrified of their effects. The United States and the Soviet Union spent billions of dollars in a nuclear arms race.

A mushroom cloud rises from a test atomic explosion; the cloud is formed by a mass of hot, rising gases.

Atomic: A bomb that releases huge power by fusing atoms together or splitting them apart.

An atomic cannon is tested in 1953; it was intended to fire short-range nuclear missiles, but was never used in battle.

Titan missiles, stored in deep underground bunkers in the United States, were the main U.S. nuclear threat from 1962 to 1965.

MUTUALLY ASSURED DESTRUCTION

Both superpowers built enough nuclear weapons to obliterate the other. Politicians and military commanders argued that the best way to stop the enemy from launching an atomic strike was to have a huge nuclear arsenal. If the enemy struck, it would bring a nuclear strike in return that would destroy it.

By the 1980s, there were so many bombs that the two superpowers agreed in a series of treaties to reduce their nuclear arsenals to make the world safer. The two bombs dropped on Japan remain the only nuclear bombs ever used in warfare.

EYEWITNESS

"No issue carries more importance to the long-term health and security of humanity than the effort to reduce, and perhaps one day, rid the world of nuclear weapons."

Lawrence M. Krauss
Professor of Physics

Arsenal: A collection of weapons or a place where weapons are stored.

POLARIS

USS *George* Washington sails on the surface while on patrol.

At the end of the 1950s, the U.S. military became concerned that aircraft were becoming more vulnerable to enemy attack. They came up with a new strategy based on nuclear-armed missiles. In 1957 military authorities ordered a class of new submarines that would carry long-range strategic missiles. Eventually a number of classes of submarine were developed to carry the missiles. Together, they were all known as "boomers".

EYEWITNESS

"The Polaris firing I witnessed was a most satisfying and fascinating experience. It is still incredible to me that a missile can be successfully and accurately fired from beneath the sea."

John F. Kennedy
U.S. President, in 1963

Strategic: Related to the overall aims of a war or campaign, not to the immediate action.

UNDER WATER

The first of these ballistic weapons was the Polaris A1 missile. The A1 had a range of 2,500 miles (4,600 km) and could fly at up to 8,000 miles per hour (13,000 km/h). The British and Spanish let U.S. submarines use their ports. That brought the Soviet Union within range. The missiles were an important part of the deterrence against a Soviet attack.

The USS *George Washington* was one of the first Polaris submarines. It carried 12 Polaris A1s. Between 1960 and 1966, the U.S. Navy launched 41 boomers, sometimes called the "forty-one for freedom." All the subs were named after heroes from U.S. history.

A Polaris A3 missile is launched from the submerged submarine SSBN *Robert E. Lee*. The A3 replaced the A1 in 1963.

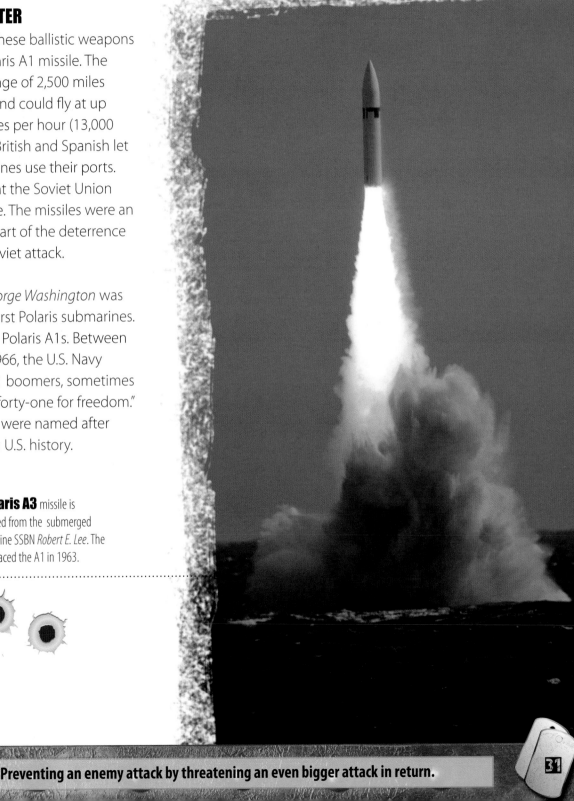

Deterrence: Preventing an enemy attack by threatening an even bigger attack in return.

RESOLUTION CLASS SUBMARINE

The *Resolution* was a British nuclear-powered submarine that gave its name to a class of just four vessels. Being closer to the front line with Eastern Europe than the United States, the British believed that they needed their own defenses. The Resolution class took over from aircraft as Britain's major nuclear deterrent. The British made a deal with their American allies that allowed the submarines to carry Polaris ballistic missiles.

HMS *Renown*, one of the four Resolution class subs, prepares to dive. Each of the vessels carried a complement of 143 people, divided into two complete crews.

Allies: Countries that cooperate with one another for defense against a shared enemy.

UNDER WATER

The Resolution submarines patrolled the seas, watching enemy subs without being detected themselves. That meant they had to stay underwater for long periods. Their engines also had to be very quiet, so that their presence was not picked up by enemy sonar. The subs patrolled 24/7, so each vessel carried two complete crews, known as Port and Starboard. The vessels were on a permanent state of alert, so they were always ready to launch a missile.

The Resolution class resembled the U.S. Lafayette class. It was designed to carry 16 A-3 Polaris missiles. Its top speed when submerged was 28.5 miles per hour (46 km/h). The Resolution class was taken out of service in 1994, when the Trident missile took over from Polaris.

Crew members stand on the deck of HMS *Resolution* during a rendezvous with a British helicopter during an exercise.

RUNNING LATE

HMS *Resolution* fired its first Polaris missile in 1968. It was part of Demonstration and Shakedown Operations (DASO). DASO is a series of tests that make sure a vessel and crew are working well. *Resolution* passed, but the missile was launched 15 milliseconds behind schedule.

Sonar: A system that locates the enemy by detecting sound waves.

SPY SATELLITES

During the Cold War, knowing what the enemy was doing could mean life or death. Both the United States and the Soviet Union had extensive spy networks. Agents passed on secrets. Listening stations deciphered radio traffic. And spy satellites looked down on enemy territory from space.

Fylingdales in northern England is a radar station set up to detect early signs of a Soviet ballistic missile attack on Europe.

Satellite: An artificial device put into orbit at very high altitudes around Earth.

This photo from a spy satellite shows a Russian Typhoon class submarine at a dock. Analysts learned how to decipher the aerial images with great accuracy.

UNCLASSIFIED
APPROVED FOR PUBLIC RELEASE
DECLASSIFIED BY DNI
13 JANUARY 2012

Modern satellites are usually used for communications purposes, such as transmitting TV signals.

THE HEXAGON PROGRAM

The Hexagon satellite program was nicknamed Big Bird. Between 1971 and 1986, 20 satellites were put into orbit. They carried super high-resolution cameras that took images of the Soviet Union, China, or any other enemy.

The film from the camera was dropped in re-entry vehicles and retrieved in mid-air by U.S. aircraft. The images were then taken to be analyzed. All this was done without the help of computers. Hexagon was the most successful spy satellite program of the Cold War.

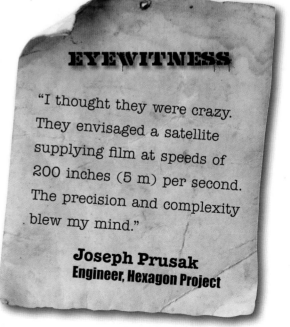

EYEWITNESS

"I thought they were crazy. They envisaged a satellite supplying film at speeds of 200 inches (5 m) per second. The precision and complexity blew my mind."

Joseph Prusak
Engineer, Hexagon Project

Re-entry vehicle: A craft designed to re-enter Earth's atmosphere from space.

Everything about the SR-71 was designed to make it invisible to enemy radar.

SR-71 BLACKBIRD

The world's fastest jet flew 16 miles (25.75 km) above Earth, on the edge of the atmosphere. At such heights, the crew had to wear spacesuits. The Blackbird could fly at Mach 3: three times the speed of sound, or 2,485 miles per hour (4,000 km/h). When it was introduced in 1966, the jet was revolutionary.

Atmosphere: The ball of gases that surrounds Earth, which stretches out toward space.

REVOLUTIONARY AIRPLANE

The Blackbird even looked different from other aircraft. Its shape was one of the first examples of "stealth technology." It was designed so that radar signals would not bounce off it and give it away. The black paint that gave the aircraft its name also helped reduce its radar profile. The paint was specially made to get rid of excess heat. Friction caused the exterior to heat up to 392°F (200°C).

The Blackbird was made of titanium and composite materials. The United States didn't have enough titanium and had to buy it from its enemy, the Soviet Union. The jet used special fuel, so its engines were specially designed and it had its own fleet of tankers.

Technicians prepare an SR-71 for a mission. The undercarriage of the SR-71 was the largest titanium object ever made.

Composite: A material made by combining other materials, such as plastics.

STRATEGIC DEFENSE INITIATIVE

In March 1983, U.S. president Ronald Reagan announced the Strategic Defense Initiative (SDI). The SDI program would build a defense shield in space to protect the United States from missile attack. The program was highly ambitious: none of the technology required existed at the time. The futuristic scheme was like something out of a sci-fi movie. It soon earned the nickname "Star Wars."

A Delta II rocket lifts off in 1989 carrying equipment for SDI tests in space.

Initiative: A step that is the first part of a new program.

In this artist's impression, satellites use ground-based laser beams to destroy targets in space.

Another artist's impression shows a satellite equipped with its own laser beam. Powering such weapons remained beyond scientific knowledge in the 1980s.

A SAFETY CURTAIN

The idea behind Star Wars was that satellites would detect any approaching ballistic missiles. Other satellites would then be used to destroy the missiles in mid-air using various types of laser or particle beams. No one knew if such technology could be created, or how long it might take.

SDI soon ran into public opposition. It was hugely expensive at a time when the Soviet threat seemed to be falling anyway. No one even knew if it would work. After costing $30 billion in research, the program was quietly abandoned.

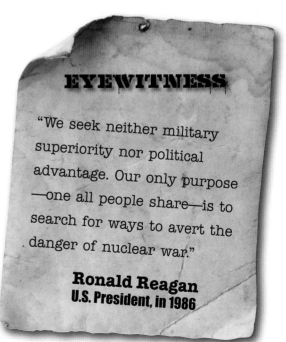

EYEWITNESS

"We seek neither military superiority nor political advantage. Our only purpose —one all people share—is to search for ways to avert the danger of nuclear war."

Ronald Reagan
U.S. President, in 1986

Laser beam: A highly concentrated beam of light that produces great energy.

TRIDENT

Trident was the third generation in the ballistic missile program. It followed Polaris and Poseidon. Launched in 1979, Trident is carried on the U.S. Navy's Ohio-class submarines. Its range is a remarkable 7,500 miles (12,000 km). But it is so accurate that even after such a journey it will arrive within a few feet of its target.

A Trident lifts off during tests in 1978; it was destroyed seconds later when its guidance system went wrong.

EYEWITNESS

"We're a friendly group of guys. We have to be; we do a lot of work in a very tight place."

Missile technician
Trident submarine

Ballistic missile: A missile that is initially powered but then falls to its target by use of gravity.

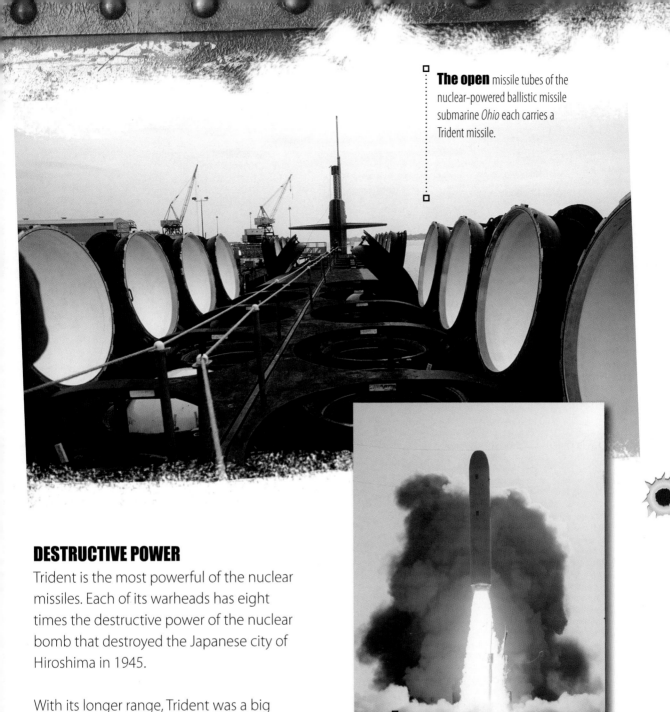

The open missile tubes of the nuclear-powered ballistic missile submarine *Ohio* each carries a Trident missile.

A Trident II missile is launched during tests in 1987; each missile can carry up to 12 nuclear warheads.

DESTRUCTIVE POWER

Trident is the most powerful of the nuclear missiles. Each of its warheads has eight times the destructive power of the nuclear bomb that destroyed the Japanese city of Hiroshima in 1945.

With its longer range, Trident was a big advance on the Poseidon. The submarines that carried Trident were bigger than Polaris and Poseidon subs; they could patrol an area ten times as large. Trident is launched from deep below the ocean's surface to the edge of space. In space, computers guide the missile to its destination.

Warhead: Part of a missile that carries the explosive charge.

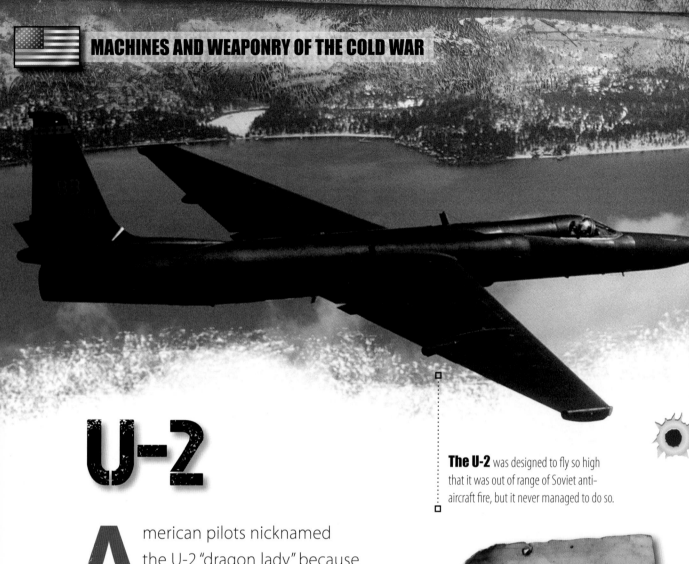

U-2

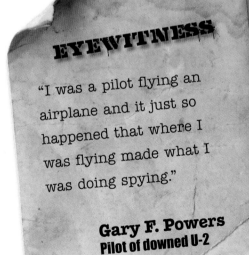

The U-2 was designed to fly so high that it was out of range of Soviet anti-aircraft fire, but it never managed to do so.

American pilots nicknamed the U-2 "dragon lady" because they said that it was hard to fly and even harder to land. The U-2 was a reconnaissance plane designed to spy on the Soviet Union. Everything about the U-2's performance was sacrificed to achieve one thing: It had to be able to fly at extreme altitudes. The jet's long, narrow wings helped it fly through the thin air at 70,000 feet (21,336 m). The spy plane was intended to fly so high that it could evade any Soviet radar, fighter, or missile.

EYEWITNESS

"I was a pilot flying an airplane and it just so happened that where I was flying made what I was doing spying."

Gary F. Powers
Pilot of downed U-2

Reconnaissance: Gathering information about enemy armed forces and movements.

Russians examine the wreckage of the U-2 shot down on May 1, 1960; the Soviet Union used the plane for propaganda.

Gary Powers was captured by the Soviets; the U.S. pilot was put on trial and forced to confess to being on a spying mission.

BALANCING ACT

The plane's design is based on that of a glider. There is little room for the pilot. He has to wear a spacesuit to fly so high, otherwise his blood would boil! The plane's balance is so sensitive that film for its camera has to be carefully positioned.

The U-2 entered service in 1957, but the Americans kept its existence secret. The "U" stood for "utility." The name didn't really mean anything, in case the Soviets got to hear about it. But on May 1, 1960, a U-2 was shot down over Soviet territory. The United States denied it even existed. But the Soviets had captured the pilot, Captain Gary Powers, so they had proof.

Glider: An airplane that does not have an engine; it flies using rising currents of air.

VULCAN BOMBER

A Vulcan pilot had one of the most dangerous jobs in Britain in the Cold War: to intercept a nuclear missile in midair. Two Vulcans were kept ready at all times, with their engines running and the pilots on board. Under the Quick Reaction Alert program, the maximum warning of a missile strike would be four minutes. The Vulcans had to get in the air and shoot the missiles down before they reached their targets.

A Vulcan takes off; its delta wings gave it more stability at high speeds.

Intercept: To stop someone or something from reaching a destination.

The probe on the nose of the Vulcan was used for midair refueling when it was attached to a hose from another airplane.

Two Vulcans fly above the radar station at Fylingdales, in northern England, which would give them warning of a missile attack.

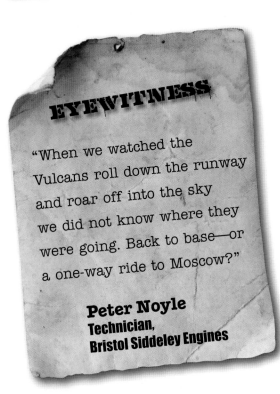

EYEWITNESS

"When we watched the Vulcans roll down the runway and roar off into the sky we did not know where they were going. Back to base—or a one-way ride to Moscow?"

Peter Noyle
Technician,
Bristol Siddeley Engines

VARIOUS DUTIES

If the Vulcan had to intercept a missile, it would do so from an altitude of 50,000 feet (15,240 m) at a range of 100–200 miles (160–320 km). Once it had fired its own missile, the Vulcan would flee as fast as possible. But the chances of the pilots escaping were slim.

The Vulcan had other tasks, too. It was part of Britain's nuclear deterrent. The delta-wing jet acted as a strategic bomber that could carry both nuclear and conventional weapons. The Vulcan flew at super-high altitudes, out of range of enemy radar or missiles. It was painted white because experts thought that gave it better camouflage at high altitudes.

Camouflage: Color schemes designed to make something more difficult to see.

GLOSSARY

ace: A pilot who has shot down a certain number of enemy aircraft.

arsenal: A collection of weapons or a place where weapons are stored.

atomic: A bomb that releases huge power by fusing atoms together or splitting them apart.

ballistic missile: A missile that is powered but then falls to its target by gravity.

camouflage: Color schemes designed to make an object more difficult to see.

class: A group of warships that are all based on the same design and specifications.

composite: A material made by combining other materials, such as plastics.

deterrence: Preventing an enemy attack by threatening an even bigger attack in return.

fallout: The spread of harmful microscopic nuclear material after an atomic explosion.

fast-attack: A type of submarine designed to strike at enemy vessels.

glider: An airplane that does not have an engine; it flies using rising currents of air.

ideology: A system of political ideas that forms the basis of a society.

interceptor: A fighter that can interrupt the flight of an enemy aircraft.

joystick: The column that controls the height and direction of an airplane.

laser beam: A highly concentrated beam of light that produces great energy.

Mach: A measure of speed relative to the speed of sound, which is Mach 1.

maneuvers: The coordinated positioning and moving around of military forces.

nuclear: A bomb that works by releasing the vast power contained in atoms.

reconnaissance: Gathering information about enemy armed forces and movements.

strategic: Related to the overall aims of a war or campaign, not to the immediate action.

Superpowers: The countries that led the sides in the Cold War: the United States and the Soviet Union.

supersonic: Traveling faster than the speed of sound, 768 miles per hour (1,236 km/h).

swept wing: A wing that is angled back, rather than sticking straight out.

torpedo: An underwater missile that has its own engine to push it through the water.

warhead: The part of a bomb that contains the detonator and the explosive.

FURTHER INFORMATION

BOOKS

Braulick, Carrie A. *U.S. Air Force Spy Planes* (Blazers Military Vehicles). Capstone Press, 2006.

Freese, Susan M. *Nuclear Weapons* (Essential Issues). Essential Library, 2011.

Green, Michael, and Gladys Green. *Tactical Fighters: The F-15 Eagles* (Edge Books). Capstone Press, 2008.

McNeese, Tim. *The Cold War and Postwar America (1946–1963)* (Discovering U.S. History). Chelsea House Publishing, 2010.

Teitelbaum, Michael. *Submarines: Underwater Stealth* (Mighty Military Machines). Enslow Publishers, 2006.

Zobel, Derek. *Nimitz Aircraft Carriers* (Torque: Military Machines). Children's Press, 2008.

WEBSITES

http://www.historylearningsite.co.uk/coldwar.htm
History Learning Site about the Cold War, including the arms race.

http://americanhistory.si.edu/subs/history/timeline/index.html
Smithsonian Institution's Museum of American History guide to submarines in the Cold War.

http://www.history.com/topics/arms-race
History.com pages about the Cold War arms race, with video and speeches.

http://www.atomicarchive.com/History/coldwar/index.shtml
National Science Digital Library's brief history of the Cold War.

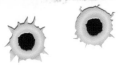

INDEX